EMMANUEL JOSEPH

The Margin of Life, Creating Space for Focus, Mindfulness, and Deeper Connections

Copyright © 2025 by Emmanuel Joseph

All rights reserved. No part of this publication may be reproduced, stored or transmitted in any form or by any means, electronic, mechanical, photocopying, recording, scanning, or otherwise without written permission from the publisher. It is illegal to copy this book, post it to a website, or distribute it by any other means without permission.

First edition

This book was professionally typeset on Reedsy.
Find out more at reedsy.com

Contents

1	Chapter 1: Introduction: The Essence of Margin	1
2	Chapter 2: The Noise of Modern Life	3
3	Chapter 3: Reclaiming Your Focus	4
4	Chapter 4: The Power of Mindfulness	5
5	Chapter 5: Building Deep Connections	6
6	Chapter 6: Creating Space in Your Daily Routine	7
7	Chapter 7: The Role of Technology	8
8	Chapter 8: Simplifying Your Environment	9
9	Chapter 9: The Benefits of Solitude	10
10	Chapter 10: Mindful Communication	11
11	Chapter 11: Nurturing Relationships	13
12	Chapter 12: The Joy of Missing Out	14
13	Chapter 13: Setting Boundaries	15
14	Chapter 14: Self-Care and Mental Health	16
15	Chapter 15: The Role of Nature	17
16	Chapter 16: Reflecting on Your Journey	18
17	Chapter 17: Conclusion: Embracing the Margin	19

1

Chapter 1: Introduction: The Essence of Margin

In the hustle and bustle of today's world, the concept of margin often gets lost. Margin is the space between our load and our limits. It is the breathing room, the pause, and the grace that allows us to live our lives fully and authentically. In this book, we will explore how creating margins in different aspects of our lives can lead to greater focus, mindfulness, and deeper connections with ourselves and others.

Margin is not just about managing our time better; it's about creating space for what truly matters. It's about saying no to the unnecessary to say yes to the essential. By embracing margin, we can reduce stress, increase productivity, and enhance our overall well-being. This chapter will set the stage for our journey toward a more focused and mindful life, rich with meaningful connections.

The journey to creating margin begins with recognizing its importance. Too often, we fill our lives to the brim, leaving no room for spontaneity, reflection, or genuine connection. By understanding the essence of margin, we can start to prioritize our lives differently. We can learn to appreciate the moments of stillness and use them to cultivate a deeper sense of purpose and fulfillment.

As we embark on this journey together, remember that creating margin is not about perfection but about progress. It's about making intentional choices that align with our values and bring us closer to our true selves. So, let's take a deep breath, embrace the space, and begin to uncover the margin of life.

2

Chapter 2: The Noise of Modern Life

Modern life is often characterized by noise—both literal and metaphorical. This noise comes in many forms: the constant notifications on our smartphones, the endless stream of information from the internet, and the societal pressures to always be busy. All this noise can be overwhelming, making it difficult to focus, be mindful, or form deep connections.

The relentless noise of modern life creates a sense of urgency that leaves little room for contemplation or relaxation. It fills our minds with clutter, making it challenging to distinguish what is truly important from what is merely urgent. To create margin, we must learn to recognize and reduce this noise, giving ourselves the gift of silence and clarity.

One way to combat the noise is to set boundaries with technology. This means consciously deciding when and how we use our devices, allowing ourselves periods of digital detox. By reducing our exposure to constant notifications and information overload, we can create space for more meaningful activities and interactions.

Another way to reduce noise is to simplify our environments. This can involve decluttering our physical spaces, minimizing distractions, and creating a serene atmosphere that promotes relaxation and focus. By curating our surroundings, we can cultivate a sense of calm that allows us to connect more deeply with ourselves and others.

3

Chapter 3: Reclaiming Your Focus

Focus is a precious resource in a world full of distractions. Reclaiming our focus means taking control of our attention and directing it toward what truly matters. This chapter will explore strategies for enhancing focus, such as setting clear priorities, managing our time effectively, and practicing mindfulness techniques.

To reclaim our focus, we must first identify the sources of distraction in our lives. These distractions can be external, like noisy environments and digital interruptions, or internal, like wandering thoughts and emotional turbulence. By recognizing these distractions, we can take steps to minimize their impact and create a more conducive environment for concentration.

Setting clear priorities is essential for maintaining focus. This involves distinguishing between urgent and important tasks, and allocating our time and energy accordingly. By focusing on what truly matters, we can avoid the trap of busyness and make meaningful progress toward our goals.

Mindfulness practices, such as meditation and deep breathing exercises, can also help us reclaim our focus. These techniques train our minds to stay present and attentive, reducing the influence of distractions. By incorporating mindfulness into our daily routines, we can enhance our ability to concentrate and bring greater intention to our actions.

4

Chapter 4: The Power of Mindfulness

Mindfulness is the practice of being fully present and engaged in the current moment. It allows us to experience life more deeply, appreciate the little things, and respond to challenges with greater clarity and calmness. In this chapter, we will explore the benefits of mindfulness and how to incorporate it into our daily lives.

One of the primary benefits of mindfulness is that it helps reduce stress. By focusing on the present moment, we can let go of worries about the past or future. This can lead to a greater sense of peace and well-being. Mindfulness also improves our ability to concentrate, making it easier to stay focused on tasks and make better decisions.

Incorporating mindfulness into our daily lives doesn't require a significant time commitment. Simple practices like mindful breathing, paying attention to our senses, and taking mindful walks can make a big difference. These activities help ground us in the present and cultivate a sense of gratitude for the world around us.

Mindfulness also enhances our relationships by helping us become better listeners and more empathetic. When we are fully present with others, we can connect with them on a deeper level and respond to their needs more effectively. By practicing mindfulness, we create space for more meaningful and fulfilling interactions.

5

Chapter 5: Building Deep Connections

Deep connections with others are essential for our emotional and mental well-being. In this chapter, we will explore how to cultivate and maintain these connections in a world that often prioritizes superficial interactions.

Building deep connections begins with being genuinely interested in others. This means taking the time to listen, ask questions, and show empathy. By being present and attentive, we can create a safe and supportive environment where others feel valued and understood.

Vulnerability is another key component of deep connections. When we open up and share our thoughts and feelings with others, we create opportunities for intimacy and trust. While it can be challenging to be vulnerable, it is essential for forming authentic and meaningful relationships.

Maintaining deep connections also requires effort and intention. This means regularly reaching out to loved ones, making time for meaningful conversations, and being there for each other during difficult times. By prioritizing our relationships and nurturing them, we can create a strong support network that enriches our lives.

6

Chapter 6: Creating Space in Your Daily Routine

Creating space in our daily routines is essential for maintaining focus, mindfulness, and deep connections. In this chapter, we will explore strategies for decluttering our schedules and making time for what truly matters.

One effective strategy is to simplify our commitments. This means learning to say no to activities and obligations that don't align with our priorities. By being selective about how we spend our time, we can free up space for more meaningful and fulfilling pursuits.

Another important aspect of creating space is establishing healthy boundaries. This involves setting limits on how much time we spend on work, social media, and other distractions. By creating clear boundaries, we can protect our time and energy for activities that nourish our minds and bodies.

Incorporating moments of rest and relaxation into our daily routines is also crucial. This can include activities like meditation, reading, or spending time in nature. By making time for rest, we can recharge our batteries and maintain our overall well-being.

7

Chapter 7: The Role of Technology

Technology plays a significant role in our lives, offering both benefits and challenges. In this chapter, we will explore how to use technology mindfully and create a healthy balance between digital and offline activities.

One of the key benefits of technology is that it enables us to stay connected with others. Social media, messaging apps, and video calls allow us to maintain relationships even when we are physically apart. However, it is essential to use these tools mindfully and not let them dominate our lives.

Setting boundaries with technology is crucial for maintaining focus and mindfulness. This can include establishing specific times for checking emails and social media, turning off notifications, and creating tech-free zones in our homes. By being intentional about how we use technology, we can create space for more meaningful activities.

Another important aspect of mindful technology use is being aware of how it affects our mental and emotional well-being. This means recognizing when we need a break from screens and taking time to unplug and recharge. By prioritizing our well-being, we can create a healthier relationship with technology.

8

Chapter 8: Simplifying Your Environment

Our physical environment has a significant impact on our mental and emotional well-being. In this chapter, we will explore the importance of simplifying our surroundings and how to create a space that fosters focus, mindfulness, and deeper connections.

A cluttered environment can lead to a cluttered mind. When our physical space is filled with unnecessary items, it can be challenging to concentrate and feel at peace. By decluttering and organizing our surroundings, we can create a sense of order and calm that promotes well-being.

One way to simplify your environment is to adopt a minimalist mindset. This involves letting go of items that no longer serve a purpose or bring joy. By keeping only what is essential and meaningful, we can create a space that reflects our values and priorities.

Creating a serene atmosphere is also important for fostering focus and mindfulness. This can include incorporating elements of nature, such as plants and natural light, and using calming colors and textures. By designing a space that feels inviting and peaceful, we can enhance our ability to be present and mindful.

9

Chapter 9: The Benefits of Solitude

Solitude is often undervalued in a world that celebrates constant connectivity and social interaction. In this chapter, we will explore the benefits of solitude and how to create space for it in our lives.

Solitude provides an opportunity for self-reflection and introspection. When we spend time alone, we can gain a deeper understanding of our thoughts, feelings, and desires. This self-awareness is essential for personal growth and can help us make more intentional choices in our lives.

Spending time in solitude also allows us to recharge and rejuvenate. In the absence of external stimuli, we can rest our minds and bodies, reducing stress and increasing our overall well-being. By prioritizing solitude, we can maintain a healthy balance between social interaction and personal time.

Creating space for solitude requires setting boundaries and making intentional choices. This can involve scheduling regular alone time, finding a quiet place for reflection, and disconnecting from digital devices. By embracing solitude, we can cultivate a sense of inner peace and clarity that enhances our ability to connect with others.

10

Chapter 10: Mindful Communication

Effective communication is essential for building deep connections and fostering understanding. In this chapter, we will explore the principles of mindful communication and how to practice them in our interactions with others.

Mindful communication begins with active listening. This means being fully present and attentive when someone is speaking, without interrupting or judging. By truly listening, we can understand others' perspectives and respond with empathy and compassion.

Another important aspect of mindful communication is expressing ourselves clearly and honestly. This involves being aware of our words and tone, and choosing language that reflects our true thoughts and feelings. By communicating authentically, we can build trust and create deeper connections.

Mindful communication also involves being aware of nonverbal cues, such as body language and facial expressions. These cues can provide valuable information about others' emotions and intentions. By paying attention to nonverbal signals, we can enhance our understanding and respond more effectively.

Practicing mindful communication requires patience and intention. It involves slowing down, being present, and making a conscious effort to connect with others on a deeper level. By prioritizing mindful communication, we can create more meaningful and fulfilling relationships.

11

Chapter 11: Nurturing Relationships

Nurturing relationships is essential for our emotional and mental well-being. In this chapter, we will explore how to cultivate and maintain strong, healthy connections with others.

One key aspect of nurturing relationships is showing appreciation and gratitude. This means expressing our thanks and acknowledging the positive qualities and actions of others. By showing appreciation, we can strengthen our bonds and create a positive atmosphere in our relationships.

Another important aspect is providing support and encouragement. This involves being there for others during difficult times, offering a listening ear, and providing words of encouragement. By offering support, we can build trust and create a sense of security in our relationships.

Quality time is also crucial for nurturing relationships. This means setting aside time to spend with loved ones, engaging in meaningful activities, and creating shared experiences. By prioritizing quality time, we can deepen our connections and create lasting memories.

Maintaining healthy relationships also requires effective communication and conflict resolution. This involves addressing issues openly and honestly, finding common ground, and working together to find solutions. By communicating effectively, we can navigate challenges and strengthen our relationships.

12

Chapter 12: The Joy of Missing Out

In a world that celebrates constant activity and engagement, the concept of missing out can feel unsettling. However, embracing the joy of missing out (JOMO) can lead to a more fulfilling and balanced life. In this chapter, we will explore the benefits of JOMO and how to incorporate it into our daily lives.

JOMO is about finding contentment in being present and appreciating the moment, rather than constantly seeking new experiences or trying to keep up with others. It involves letting go of the fear of missing out (FOMO) and recognizing that our worth is not determined by our level of activity or social validation.

One way to embrace JOMO is to prioritize activities that bring genuine joy and fulfillment. This means focusing on what truly matters to us and letting go of the need to compare ourselves to others. By being intentional about our choices, we can create a more meaningful and satisfying life.

Another important aspect of JOMO is learning to be comfortable with solitude and downtime. This involves appreciating the value of rest and relaxation, and recognizing that it is essential for our well-being. By embracing stillness and slowing down, we can cultivate a deeper sense of inner peace and contentment.

13

Chapter 13: Setting Boundaries

Setting boundaries is essential for maintaining focus, mindfulness, and healthy relationships. In this chapter, we will explore the importance of boundaries and how to establish them in various aspects of our lives.

Boundaries help protect our time, energy, and well-being. They allow us to prioritize our needs and values, and prevent us from becoming overwhelmed by external demands. Setting boundaries involves recognizing our limits and communicating them clearly to others.

One key area where boundaries are important is in our use of technology. This can include setting limits on screen time, establishing tech-free zones, and creating specific times for checking emails and social media. By setting boundaries with technology, we can create space for more meaningful activities and interactions.

Boundaries are also crucial in our relationships. This means being clear about our needs and expectations, and not being afraid to say no when necessary. By setting boundaries with others, we can create healthier and more respectful relationships.

Establishing boundaries requires self-awareness and assertiveness. It involves recognizing when we need to set limits and communicating them in a respectful and confident manner. By setting boundaries, we can create a more balanced and fulfilling life.

14

Chapter 14: Self-Care and Mental Health

Self-care is essential for maintaining our mental and emotional well-being. In this chapter, we will explore the importance of self-care and how to incorporate it into our daily routines.

Self-care involves taking intentional actions to care for our physical, mental, and emotional health. This can include activities like exercise, healthy eating, getting enough sleep, and engaging in hobbies and activities that bring joy and relaxation. By prioritizing self-care, we can enhance our overall well-being and resilience.

Mental health is a crucial aspect of self-care. This involves recognizing and addressing our emotional needs, seeking support when necessary, and engaging in practices that promote mental well-being. Mindfulness, meditation, and therapy are all valuable tools for maintaining mental health.

Creating space for self-care requires setting boundaries and making intentional choices. This means recognizing when we need to rest and recharge, and not feeling guilty about taking time for ourselves. By prioritizing self-care, we can create a more balanced and fulfilling life.

Self-care also involves being kind and compassionate toward ourselves. This means letting go of perfectionism, being patient with ourselves, and recognizing that it is okay to ask for help. By practicing self-compassion, we can cultivate a more positive and supportive relationship with ourselves.

15

Chapter 15: The Role of Nature

Nature plays a significant role in promoting our well-being and enhancing our sense of connection. In this chapter, we will explore the benefits of spending time in nature and how to incorporate it into our daily lives.

Spending time in nature has been shown to reduce stress, improve mood, and enhance overall well-being. Whether it's taking a walk in the park, hiking in the mountains, or simply enjoying the beauty of a garden, nature provides a sense of peace and tranquility that can be difficult to find in our busy lives.

Incorporating nature into our daily routines doesn't require a significant time commitment. Simple activities like spending time in the garden, going for a walk, or even bringing nature indoors with plants and natural elements can make a big difference. By making time for nature, we can enhance our physical, mental, and emotional health.

Nature also provides an opportunity for mindfulness and reflection. When we spend time in nature, we can practice being present and appreciating the beauty and wonder of the natural world. This can help us cultivate a sense of gratitude and connection to something greater than ourselves.

Creating space for nature requires intentional choices and a commitment to prioritizing our well-being. By making time for nature and incorporating it into our daily lives, we can create a more balanced and fulfilling life.

16

Chapter 16: Reflecting on Your Journey

Reflection is a powerful tool for personal growth and self-awareness. In this chapter, we will explore the importance of reflection and how to incorporate it into our daily lives.

Reflection allows us to pause and evaluate our experiences, thoughts, and actions. By taking the time to reflect, we can gain insights into our behavior, identify patterns, and make more intentional choices. Reflection helps us learn from our experiences and grow as individuals.

One way to incorporate reflection into our daily lives is to establish a regular journaling practice. Writing down our thoughts and feelings can help us process our experiences and gain clarity. By keeping a journal, we can track our progress, set goals, and celebrate our achievements.

Another important aspect of reflection is seeking feedback from others. This involves being open to constructive criticism and using it to improve ourselves. By listening to others' perspectives, we can gain valuable insights and make positive changes in our lives.

Reflection also requires making time for introspection and contemplation. This can involve setting aside quiet moments for meditation, prayer, or simply sitting in stillness. By creating space for reflection, we can cultivate a deeper understanding of ourselves and our journey.

17

Chapter 17: Conclusion: Embracing the Margin

As we conclude our journey through "The Margin of Life," we have explored various ways to create space for focus, mindfulness, and deeper connections. Embracing the margin is about making intentional choices that align with our values and priorities. It is about finding balance and creating a life that is rich with meaning and fulfillment.

Embracing the margin involves letting go of the unnecessary and focusing on what truly matters. It is about creating space for rest, reflection, and connection. By prioritizing our well-being and making intentional choices, we can create a life that is more balanced, mindful, and fulfilling.

Book Description:

In a world that celebrates constant activity and engagement, "**The Margin of Life: Creating Space for Focus, Mindfulness, and Deeper Connections**" offers a refreshing perspective on the importance of creating space in our lives. This book explores the concept of margin—the space between our load and our limits—and how it can lead to greater focus, mindfulness, and deeper connections with ourselves and others.

Through insightful chapters, the author delves into the noise of modern life, the power of mindfulness, and the benefits of solitude. Readers will learn practical strategies for reclaiming focus, setting boundaries, and nurturing relationships. The book also highlights the role of technology, the importance of self-care, and the value of spending time in nature.

"The Margin of Life" is a guide to living more intentionally and authentically. It encourages readers to let go of the unnecessary and prioritize what truly matters. By embracing the margin, readers can create a life that is rich with meaning, balance, and fulfillment.

Whether you are seeking to reduce stress, enhance your well-being, or cultivate deeper connections, "The Margin of Life" provides valuable insights and practical tips to help you create the space you need to thrive.

www.ingramcontent.com/pod-product-compliance
Lightning Source LLC
LaVergne TN
LVHW020509080526
838202LV00057B/6252